dabble lab

PAPER AIRPLANES
with a SIDE of SCIENCE

AIR SHARK!

NOVICE-LEVEL
Paper Airplanes
by Marie Buckingham

4D An Augmented Reading
Paper-Folding Experience

CAPSTONE PRESS
a capstone imprint

TABLE OF

CONTENTS

TIME TO FLY

Welcome to the cockpit! You've passed flight school and earned your seat
next to the pilot. Now it's time to get a feel for those flight controls.
While you're folding your airplanes, be sure to check the lightbulb
boxes tucked alongside the instructions for bite-size explanations
of flight-science concepts related to your models. Check the
photo boxes for tips on how to best launch your finished planes.
Remember, there are four main forces that airplanes need to fly
successfully: lift, weight, thrust, and drag. But the eight paper
airplanes in this book need one more thing: YOU!

MATERIALS

Every paper airplane builder needs a well-stocked toolbox. The models in this book use the materials listed below. Take a minute before you begin folding to gather what you need:

Paper — Any paper you can fold will work. Notebook paper is always popular. But paper with cool colors and designs gives your planes style.

Scissors — Keep a scissors handy. Some models need a snip here or there to fly well.

Clear Tape — Most paper airplanes don't need tape. But when they do, you'll be glad you have it ready to go.

TECHNIQUES AND TERMS

Folding paper airplanes isn't difficult when you understand common folding techniques and terms. Review this list before folding the models in this book. Remember to refer back to this list if you get stuck on a tricky step.

Valley Folds

Valley folds are represented by a dashed line. The paper is creased along the line. The top surface of the paper is folded against itself like a book.

Mountain Folds

Mountain folds are represented by a pink or white dashed and dotted line. The paper is creased along the line and folded behind.

Reverse Folds

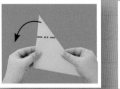  

Reverse folds are made by opening a pocket slightly and folding the model inside itself along existing creases.

Mark Folds

Mark folds are light folds used to make reference creases for a later step. Ideally, a mark fold will not be seen in the finished model.

Rabbit Ear Folds

 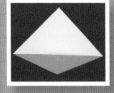

Rabbit ear folds are formed by bringing two edges of a point together using existing creases. The new point is folded to one side.

Squash Folds

Squash folds are formed by lifting one edge of a pocket and reforming it so the spine gets flattened. The existing creases become new edges.

FOLDING SYMBOLS

Fold the paper in the direction of the arrow.

Fold the paper behind.

Fold the paper and then unfold it.

Turn the paper over or rotate it to a new position.

• • • • • • • • • • • • • •

A fold or edge hidden under another layer of paper; also used to mark where to cut with a scissors

★ AIR SHARK

Traditional Model

Prowl the skies with your very own Air Shark.
This sturdy plane has a smooth, steady glide.
It's a paper predator that's always ready to hunt.

Materials

* 8.5- by 11-inch (22- by 28-centimeter) paper

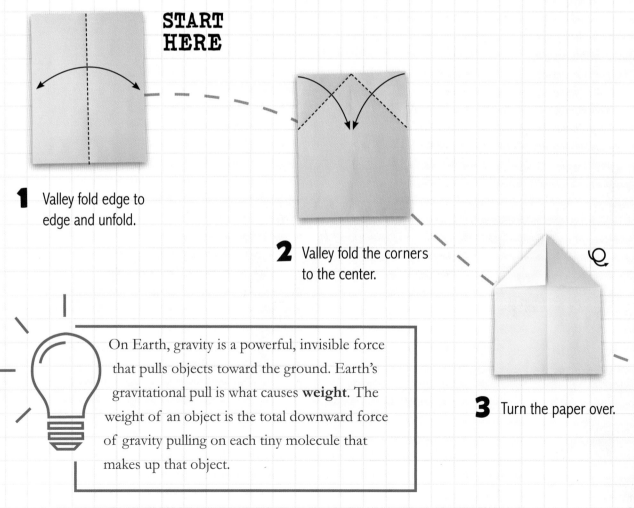

START HERE

1 Valley fold edge to edge and unfold.

2 Valley fold the corners to the center.

3 Turn the paper over.

On Earth, gravity is a powerful, invisible force that pulls objects toward the ground. Earth's gravitational pull is what causes **weight**. The weight of an object is the total downward force of gravity pulling on each tiny molecule that makes up that object.

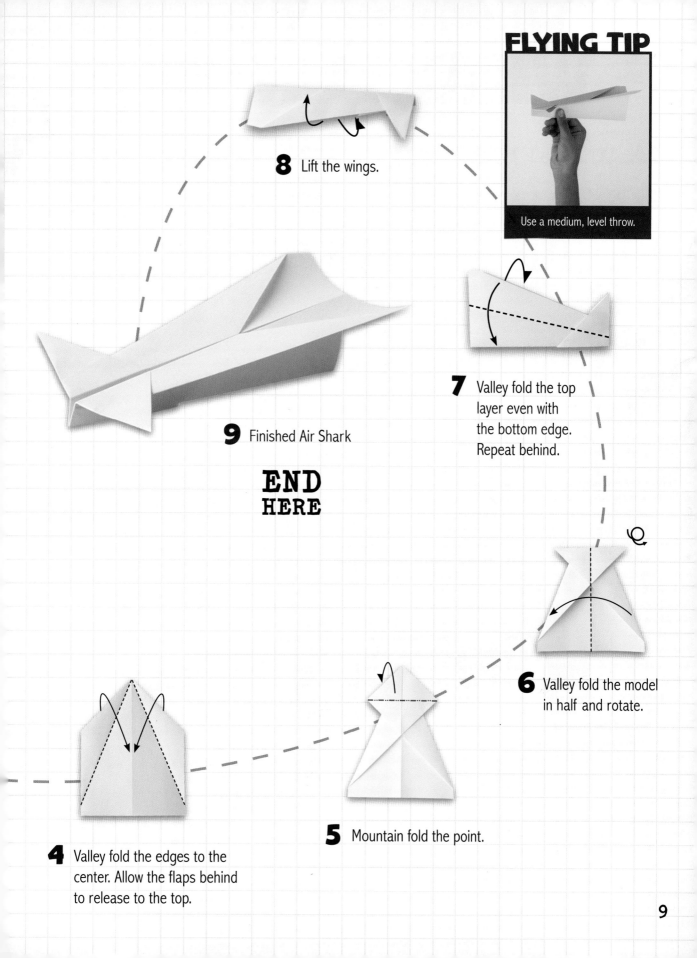

8 Lift the wings.

7 Valley fold the top layer even with the bottom edge. Repeat behind.

9 Finished Air Shark

END
HERE

6 Valley fold the model in half and rotate.

5 Mountain fold the point.

4 Valley fold the edges to the center. Allow the flaps behind to release to the top.

⭐ WIND TUNNEL

Traditional Model

The Wind Tunnel takes paper airplanes in a very
different direction. This circular wing is thrown like
a football. Get your arm warmed up. You'll be amazed
by how far this tube will glide through the air.

Materials

* 8.5- by 11-inch (22- by 28-cm) paper
* scissors
* tape

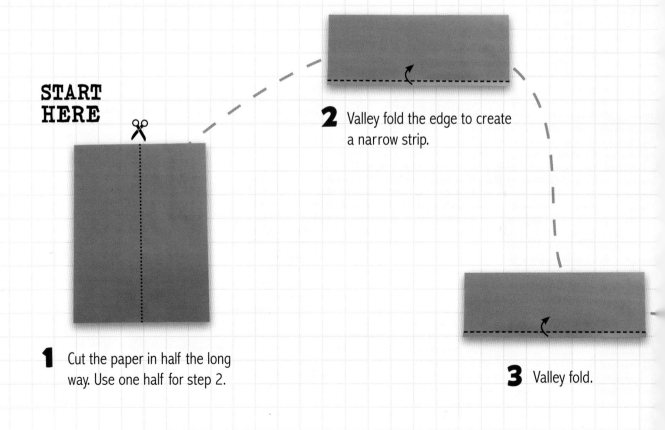

START HERE

2 Valley fold the edge to create a narrow strip.

1 Cut the paper in half the long way. Use one half for step 2.

3 Valley fold.

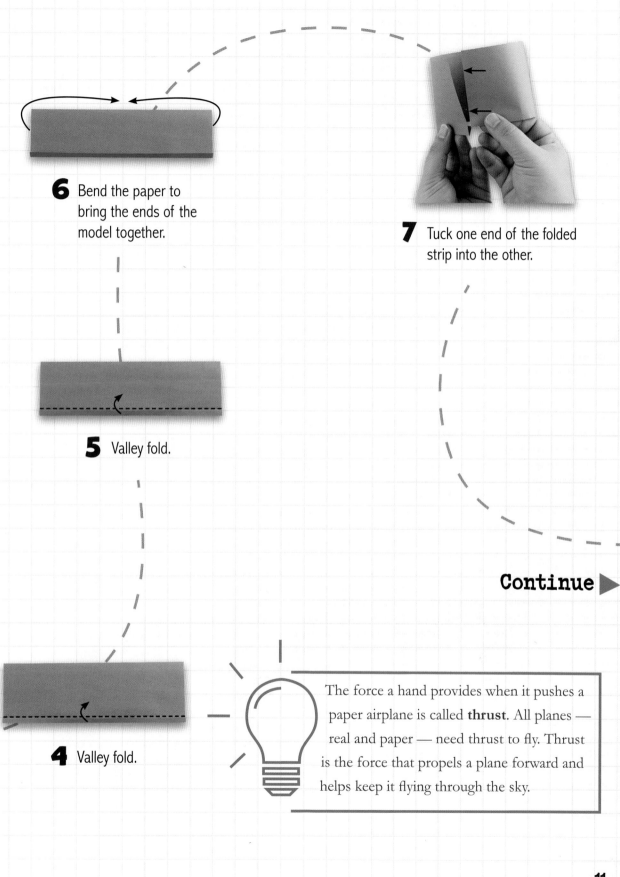

6 Bend the paper to bring the ends of the model together.

7 Tuck one end of the folded strip into the other.

5 Valley fold.

Continue ▶

4 Valley fold.

The force a hand provides when it pushes a paper airplane is called **thrust**. All planes — real and paper — need thrust to fly. Thrust is the force that propels a plane forward and helps keep it flying through the sky.

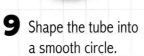

9 Shape the tube into a smooth circle.

10 Finished Wind Tunnel

END HERE

8 Tape the seam to hold the model together.

FLYING TIP

Cup the model in your hand with the folded strip facing forward. Use a hard spiral throw as if you were throwing a football.

STREAKING EAGLE

Traditional Model

The Strcaking Eagle combines style and mechanics. Sleek wing flaps help the plane fly straight. Elevators let you control how the plane rises or dives.

Materials

* 8.5- by 11-inch (22- by 28-cm) paper
* scissors

Continue ▶

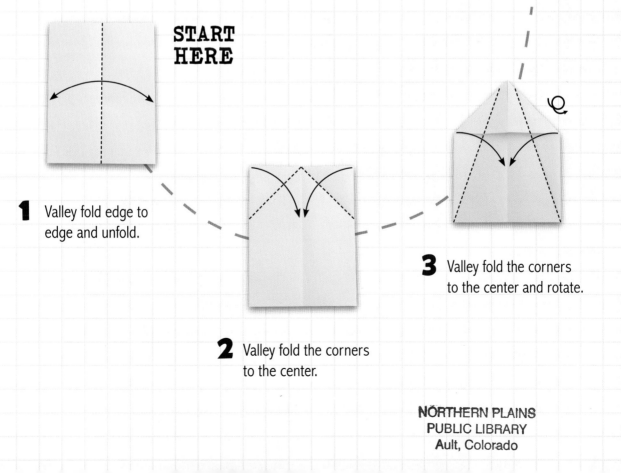

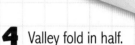

START HERE

1 Valley fold edge to edge and unfold.

2 Valley fold the corners to the center.

3 Valley fold the corners to the center and rotate.

4 Valley fold in half.

During flight, a pilot controls the movable surface on an airplane's tail called an **elevator**. The elevator moves an airplane's nose up or down. When the elevator is pushed down, the airplane's nose will move down. When the elevator is pulled up, the aircraft's nose will move up.

5 Valley fold the top layer. Repeat behind.

6 Valley fold the edge of the wing. Repeat behind.

7 Lift the wings.

10 Finished Streaking Eagle

END
HERE

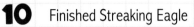

9 Cut a flap in the back of each wing. Angle the flaps (elevators) upward slightly.

8 Lift the wing flaps so they stand up at 90-degree angles.

FLYING TIP

Use a medium, level throw. Adjust the flaps to control the flight path.

# WHISPER DART

Designed by Christopher L. Harbo

The Whisper Dart looks like a simple paper airplane. But extra folds give it added weight in the nose. Got your eye on a target across the room? This design will deliver!

Materials

* 8.5- by 11-inch (22- by 28-cm) paper

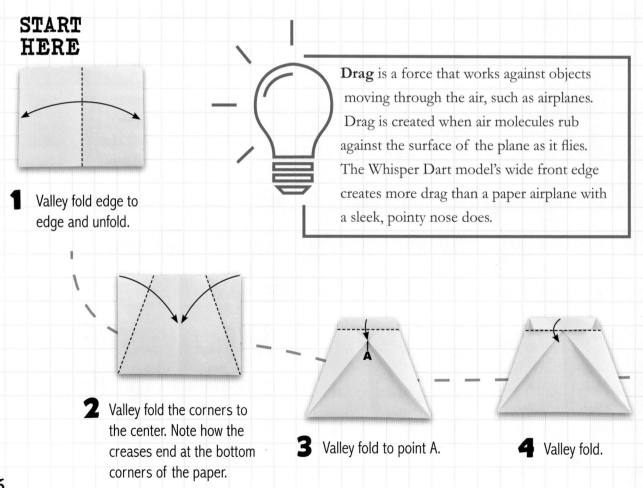

START HERE

1 Valley fold edge to edge and unfold.

Drag is a force that works against objects moving through the air, such as airplanes. Drag is created when air molecules rub against the surface of the plane as it flies. The Whisper Dart model's wide front edge creates more drag than a paper airplane with a sleek, pointy nose does.

2 Valley fold the corners to the center. Note how the creases end at the bottom corners of the paper.

3 Valley fold to point A.

4 Valley fold.

16

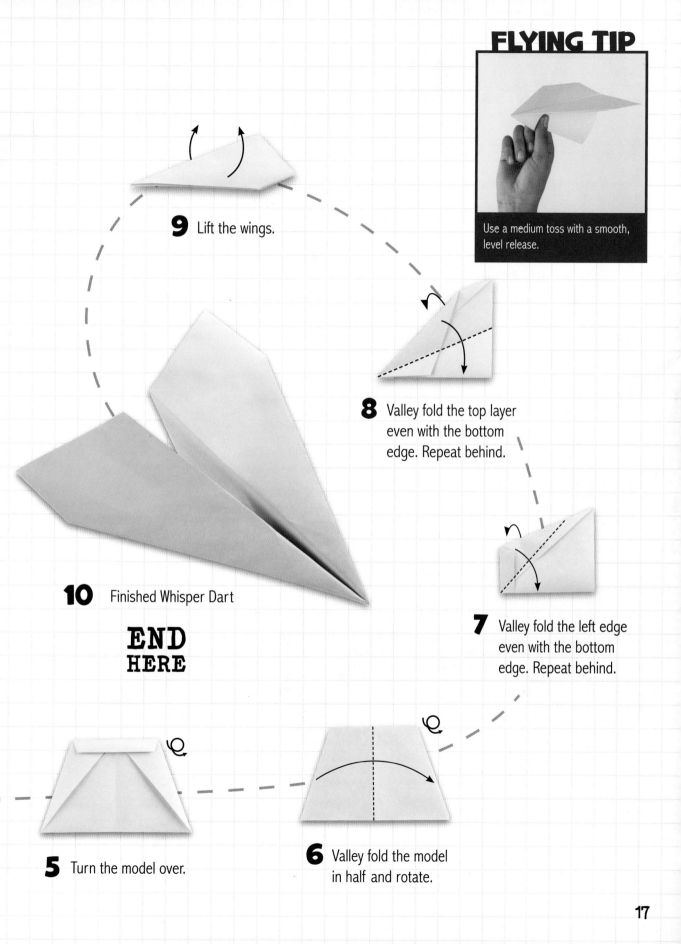

Use a medium toss with a smooth, level release.

9 Lift the wings.

8 Valley fold the top layer even with the bottom edge. Repeat behind.

7 Valley fold the left edge even with the bottom edge. Repeat behind.

10 Finished Whisper Dart

END HERE

5 Turn the model over.

6 Valley fold the model in half and rotate.

VAMPIRE BAT

Traditional Model

The Vampire Bat's flight path is a jaw-dropper. This amazing wing soars and swoops when thrown correctly. Folding it is easy. Finding a room large enough to fly it in may be a challenge.

Materials

* 8.5- by 11-inch (22- by 28-cm) paper

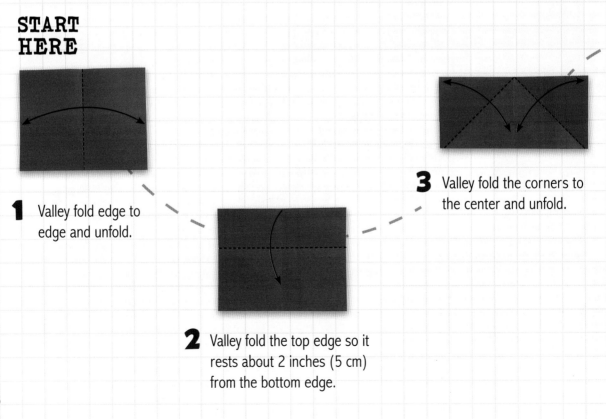

START HERE

1 Valley fold edge to edge and unfold.

2 Valley fold the top edge so it rests about 2 inches (5 cm) from the bottom edge.

3 Valley fold the corners to the center and unfold.

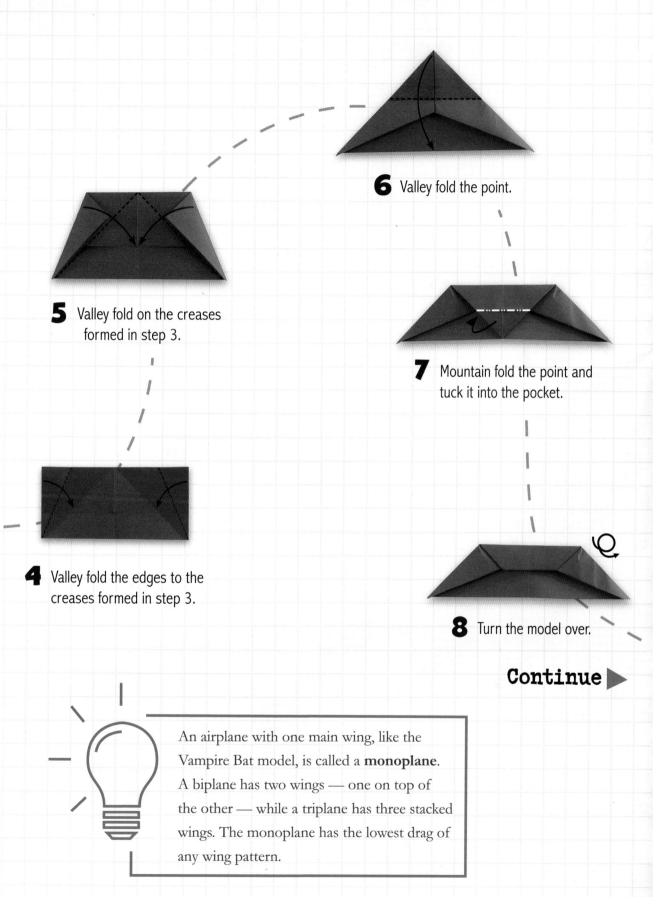

6 Valley fold the point.

5 Valley fold on the creases formed in step 3.

7 Mountain fold the point and tuck it into the pocket.

4 Valley fold the edges to the creases formed in step 3.

8 Turn the model over.

Continue ▶

An airplane with one main wing, like the Vampire Bat model, is called a **monoplane**. A biplane has two wings — one on top of the other — while a triplane has three stacked wings. The monoplane has the lowest drag of any wing pattern.

FLYING TIP

Pinch the back of the wing with two fingers and your thumb so the model forms a "V." Raise the model above your head and release with a strong forward flick of the wrist.

END HERE

11 Finished Vampire Bat

9 Mountain fold the wings and unfold slightly.

10 Valley fold the wing tips and unfold slightly.

⭐ ARROWHEAD

Traditional Model

Get ready to soar! The Arrowhead is a flying champion.
This plane can cover amazing distances with very little
effort. You'll get your exercise chasing this model from
one end of the room to the other.

Materials

* 8.5- by 11-inch (22- by 28-cm) paper

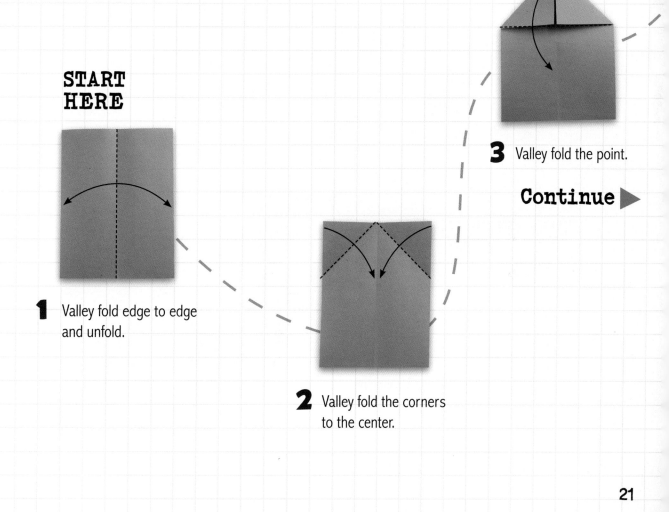

**START
HERE**

1 Valley fold edge to edge
and unfold.

2 Valley fold the corners
to the center.

3 Valley fold the point.

Continue ▶

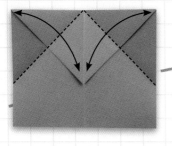

4 Valley fold the corners to the center and unfold.

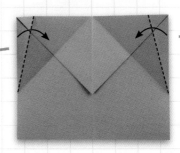

5 Valley fold the corners. Note that the creases end at the creases made in step 4.

12 Finished Arrowhead

END HERE

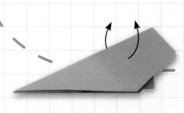

11 Lift the wings.

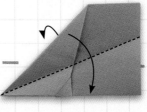

10 Valley fold the top flap even with the bottom edge. Repeat behind.

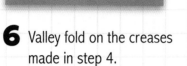

6 Valley fold on the creases made in step 4.

An airplane needs an upward force called **lift** to fly. Wings create lift as air flows over them during flight. Airplane wings are usually curved. Air molecules moving over the wing's top, curved surface travel faster than molecules moving along the wing's flat bottom. The slower-moving air molecules beneath the wing create a high amount of pressure and create lift.

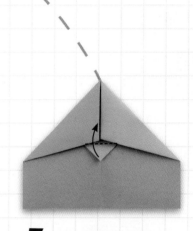

7 Valley fold the point.

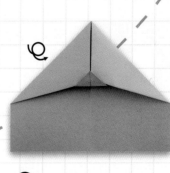

8 Turn the model over.

9 Valley fold the model in half and rotate.

⭐ NIGHTHAWK

Traditional Model

The Nighthawk is a great flier with a simple design. This classic glider isn't fancy, but its graceful flight is sure to impress. Make two planes and challenge a friend to a flight contest.

Materials

* 8.5- by 11-inch (22- by 28-cm) paper

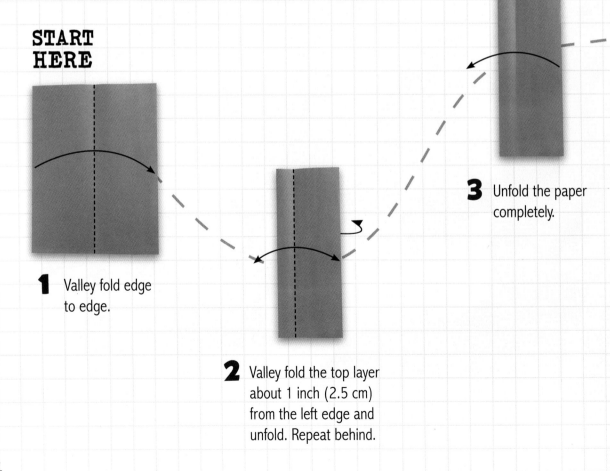

START HERE

1 Valley fold edge to edge.

2 Valley fold the top layer about 1 inch (2.5 cm) from the left edge and unfold. Repeat behind.

3 Unfold the paper completely.

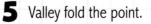

5 Valley fold the point.

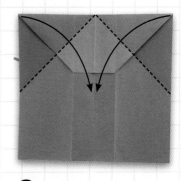

6 Valley fold the corners to the center crease.

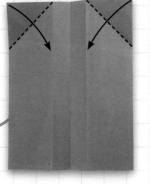

4 Valley fold the corners to the creases made in step 2.

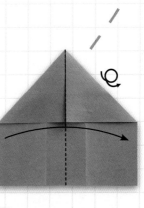

7 Valley fold the model in half and rotate.

A **glider** is a small plane without an engine. It's often towed into the air by a rope connected to a motorized plane, then released into the sky. A glider uses air currents called thermals to stay aloft for hours. Thermals are special columns of warm, rising air, created by the sun's rays heating Earth's surface. Thermals push up on a glider's wings and keep it in flight.

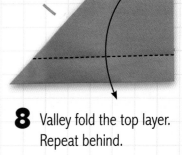

8 Valley fold the top layer. Repeat behind.

Continue ▶

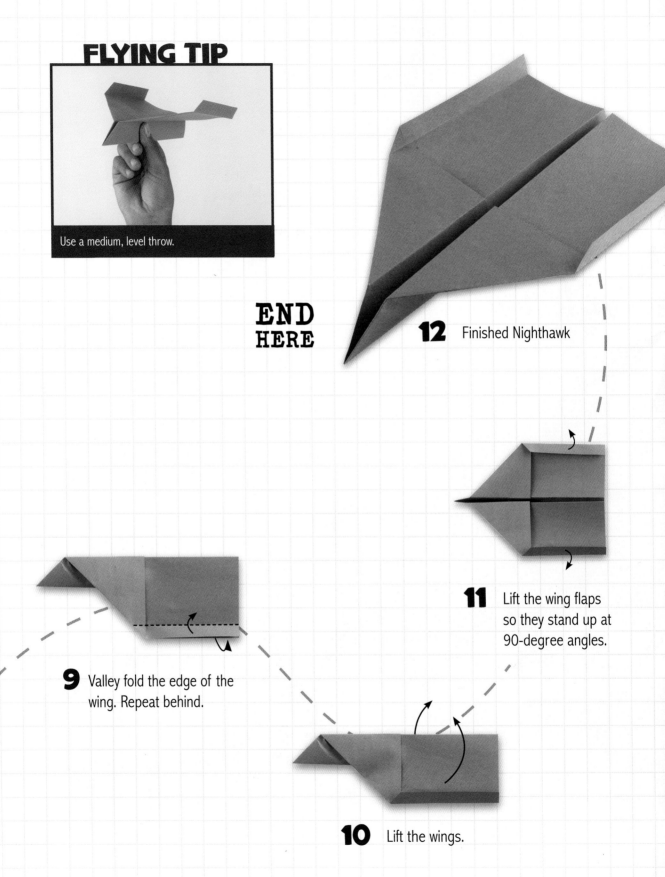

Use a medium, level throw.

END HERE

12 Finished Nighthawk

11 Lift the wing flaps so they stand up at 90-degree angles.

9 Valley fold the edge of the wing. Repeat behind.

10 Lift the wings.

26

VAPOR

Designed by Christopher L. Harbo

The Vapor has extra folds in the nose for strength and balance. The wing flaps guide the plane on an even flight. With very little effort, this model will slip silently from your hand and arc across the room.

Materials

* 8.5- by 11-inch (22- by 28-cm) paper

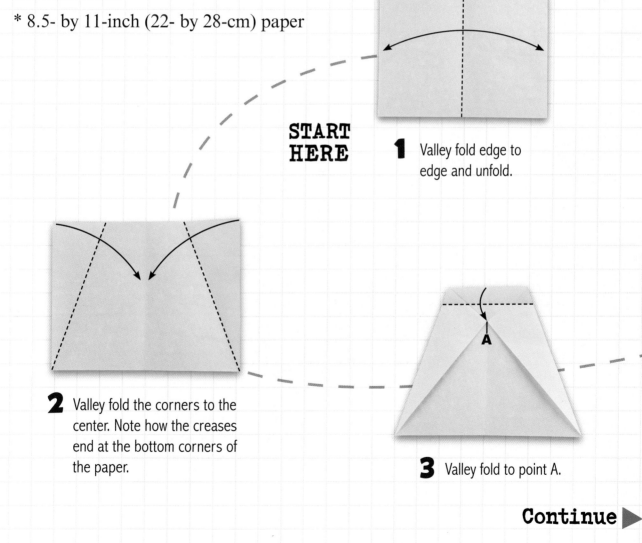

START HERE

1 Valley fold edge to edge and unfold.

2 Valley fold the corners to the center. Note how the creases end at the bottom corners of the paper.

3 Valley fold to point A.

Continue ▶

5 Valley fold the corners to the center.

6 Valley fold the model in half and rotate.

An airplane in flight rotates along three lines, or axes: lateral, vertical, and longitudinal. Movement along the lateral axis (which runs from wing to wing) is called **pitch**. The nose moves up or down. Movement along the vertical axis (which runs through the center of the plane) is called **yaw.** The nose moves side to side. When a plane moves around the longitudinal axis (which runs from nose to tail), the plane **rolls**.

4 Turn the model over.

FLYING TIP

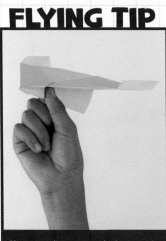

Use a medium, smooth throw with a slight upward angle.

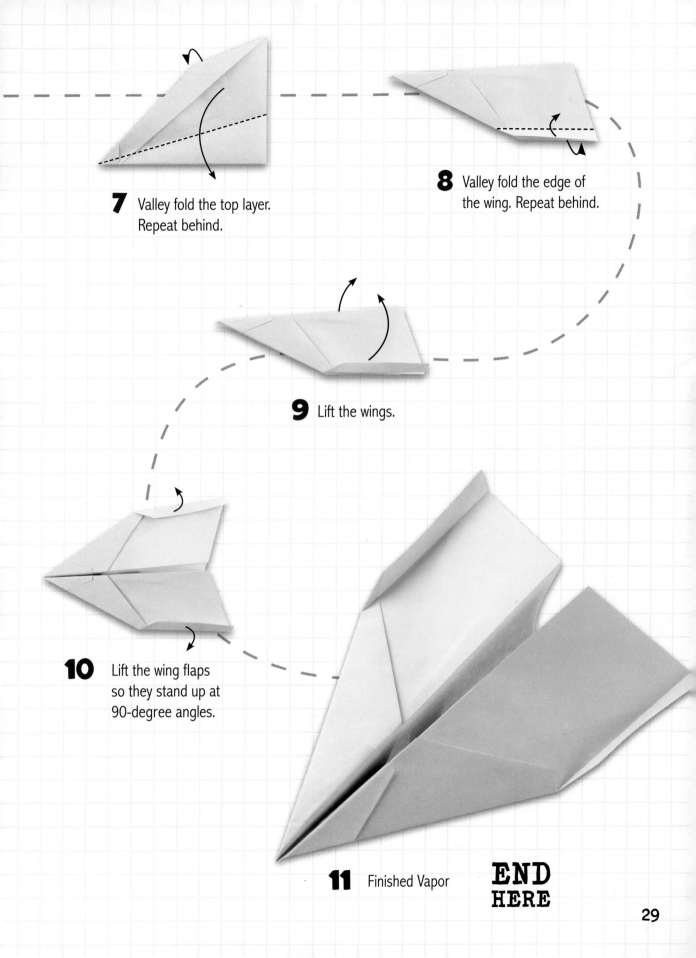

7 Valley fold the top layer. Repeat behind.

8 Valley fold the edge of the wing. Repeat behind.

9 Lift the wings.

10 Lift the wing flaps so they stand up at 90-degree angles.

11 Finished Vapor

END HERE

⭐ INSIDE THE HANGAR:
WIND TUNNELS

Engineers are people who use science and math to plan, design, or build. When creating new aircraft (or spacecraft), engineers often rely on wind tunnels to test their designs. A wind tunnel is a large tube-shaped piece of equipment. A mount in the center of the tube holds a test plane in place. When the wind tunnel is turned on, air flows around the plane like it would if the plane were flying.

Most wind tunnels have powerful fans to create high-speed winds. Air speeds in some tunnels reach 4,000 miles (6,437 kilometers) per hour — five times the speed of sound! During testing, smoke or dye may be injected into the wind so engineers can study how air flows around an airplane. Photographs of this moving air allow engineers to see how they can improve a plane's design to lower drag and increase lift.

To save money, engineers may test a smaller-scale model of a new plane design inside a smaller wind tunnel. Based on the engineers' findings, the design may be changed and tested again.

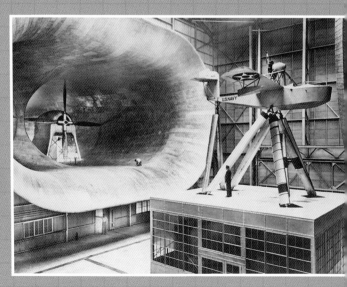

This seven-story wind tunnel was used to test airplane design in 1932.

READ MORE

Collins, John M. *The New World Champion Paper Airplane Book: Featuring the Guinness World Record-Breaking Design, with Tear-Out Planes to Fold and Fly.* New York: Ten Speed Press, 2013.

LaFosse, Michael G. *Michael LaFosse's Origami Airplanes.* North Clarendon, Vt.: Tuttle Publishing, 2016.

Lee, Kyong Hwa. *Amazing Paper Airplanes: The Craft and Science of Flight.* Albuquerque, N.Mex.: University of New Mexico Press, 2016.

INTERNET SITES

Use FactHound to find Internet sites related to this book.

Visit *www.facthound.com*

Just type in 9781543507966 and go.

Special thanks to our adviser, Polly Kadolph, Associate Professor,
University of Dubuque (Iowa) Aviation Department, for her expertise.

Dabble Lab Books are published by Capstone Press,
1710 Roe Crest Drive, North Mankato, Minnesota 56003
www.mycapstone.com

Library of Congress Cataloging-in-Publication data is available on the Library of Congress website.
ISBN: 978-1-5435-0796-6 (library binding)
ISBN: 978-1-5435-0800-0 (eBook PDF)

Summary: Coach your readers into the sky with a few basic paper folds and a side of science.
Photo-illustrated instructions and special 4D components show young flight-school students
how to build the Air Shark and other novice-level paper airplanes step-by-step. Fact-filled sidebars
and an "Inside the Hangar" feature work in tandem with the projects to explain flight concepts.

Editorial Credits
Jill Kalz, editor; Heidi Thompson, designer; Eric Gohl, media researcher; Laura Manthe, production specialist

Photo Credits
Capstone Studio: Karon Dubke, all steps
Shutterstock: design elements, Everett Historical, 30

Printed in the United States of America.
010761S18